DATE DUE

"With *My E*⋯ ⋯rafted a
work that m⋯ ⋯-hearted
and the serio⋯ ⋯ceptive-
ly quiet poen⋯ ⋯nd (per-
haps most p⋯ ⋯n of the
American pa⋯ ⋯ire, and
we are wiser⋯

⋯s
⋯glish
⋯ston

DEMCO, INC. 38-2931

1

Copyright© 1995
by Mike O'Connell

First Edition

Library of Congress Catalog Card Number: 95-95237
ISBN: 0-9640408-1-6

For additional copies of this book contact:
Hugger Mugger Publishing
E10469 Sunset Road
Baraboo, WI 53913

Printed in USA by
Palmer Publications, Inc.
Amherst, WI 54406

My Bucket's Got a Hole In It

New Poems by Mike O'Connell

ACKNOWLEDGMENTS

For the following previously published material:

Agriview for "The Cow They Couldn't Kill"

Wisconsin State Farmer for:
> "All Hail to Monsanto"
> "At the Sauk County Unemployment Office"
> "Dairy Science Christmas"
> "Seeds of Memory: Sowing Oats"

1996 Wisconsin Poets Calendar for "Applejack"

Cover photos by Ron Brayer

Page 14 photo by Ron Brayer

Pages 16 and 64 photos by Sharon O'Connell

This book is dedicated to

CARLA HAGENOW-GUNST

editor of the *Wisconsin State Farmer*, a publication which holds to the antiquated beliefs that agriculture has something to do with farmers, and that journalism has something to do with freedom of expression.

Special thanks to Sue Boshers of Word Magic for the preparation of the text and to Chris Doyle and Dick Jaworski of Amherst Press for their contributions to the format and design of this book.

CONTENTS

GENESIS—COMING HOME TO A PLACE HE'D NEVER BEEN BEFORE

How does a city boy from the East end up milking cows on a rundown farm in Wisconsin? This question, in so many words, has been posed to me countless times since my arrival in Sauk County almost thirty years ago. I am afraid I have never answered it to anyone's satisfaction, including my own. The following recollections may give some insight into what drew me to a way of life apparently so remote from the circumstances of my upbringing.

Any child, even in the ghetto of a major city, will seek out something of the "natural" world, be it no more than a remnant of prairie in a vacant lot, or a flock of pigeons on a tenement rooftop. Though the first seven years of my life were spent in what now would be termed a low income apartment project in Southeast Washington, D.C., we lived only a short block from Oxon Run, a pleasant little creek which wound its wooded way towards Southern Maryland. There I came to know the boyhood pleasures of skimming flat stones on the water and of Saturday hikes downstream with Dad, brother, and pals from the neighborhood. As Tom T. Hall has pointed out, there are really only two kinds of boys—country boys, and country boys from the city.

When I was seven my parents, with two growing sons and another on the way, began looking in earnest for a house of their own. The year was 1950. For $13,500 they purchased a new brick "rambler" twelve miles south in Prince Georges County, on a gravel road three miles east of Clinton, home of Mary Surratt. My mother still lives in the house today. Here there was still dense pine forest, tadpoles in the roadside ditches, and blackberries and poison ivy among the brambles. More important to me, there was space on our ½ acre lot for a garden. Early on I seem to have been fascinated with the miracle that is the sprouting of a seed.

From the first time I saw him wield a grubbing hoe, I decided I would have to face the fact that my father—the first American-born descendant of a long line of peasant Irish potato growers—was not going to provide the example nor expertise needed to produce any kind of vegetable crop on this side of the Atlantic. An engineer for the Navy Department, he had worked on hydrogen bomb testing in the South Pacific and nuclear reactors in Idaho, and would spend time at Cape Canaveral assisting with Vanguard satellite launches. But his idea of tilling a garden was to hack out a few shallow trenches a couple feet apart, throw in some radish seeds and onion sets, and tamp them down with the back of a hoe. The sod between the rows was left undisturbed until I returned, alone, hours after the planting, and endeavored to spade under the remaining green patches. Thirty years before it was given a name and touted by land grant agricultural colleges, my dad was practicing "minimum tillage."

Although I had never seen the magnificent western uplands of Wisconsin until my graduate school days at the U.W.-Madison in the mid-sixties, I was no stranger to America's Dairyland. Our standard two week summer vacation in the 40's and 50's consisted of a train (later an auto) trip to Chicago, my dad's home, and Waukesha, my mother's. I have no more transcendent childhood memory than that of riding in a coach car of the Milwaukee Road between Milwaukee and Waukesha, looking out wide-eyed and slack-jawed at golden Guernseys grazing the green knolls of Waukesha County. To me, at the age of five or six, it was like being given a glimpse of the Garden of Eden.

In 1950 the city of Waukesha was home to less than 20,000 people. Across the street from my grandparents, neighbors sold brown eggs provided by their backyard flock of chickens. At the end of the lane, on the grounds of the famed Moor Mud Baths, was a cow pasture. Bottled milk was delivered daily with the cream on top. The refrigerator was stocked with stinky cheese, the freezer with ice cream.

Back in Clinton, I began spending more time bouncing a basketball on the driveway than tending the tomato patch. My jump shot found its way into the basket just often enough to help me win a scholarship to Dartmouth College in Hanover, New Hampshire.

There I majored in English, read and listened to Robert Frost, and never set foot on a New England farmstead. At graduation, as a way of postponing any kind of career decision, I opted for a year of graduate school at the University of Wisconsin, a school chosen as much for its geographic location as for its academic reputation. I remember a young U.W. professor trying to convince us of his deep commitment to his post-graduate research and teaching responsibilities.

"I didn't come to Madison to lounge by the lake," he said.

I had come mostly to lounge by the lake.

At year's end, with a Master's Degree in hand, I had a notion to try teaching school and coaching basketball, as opposed to continuing in a Ph.D. program not only out of touch with reality, but out of touch with Chaucer, Shakespeare, and Hawthorne as well. One of the boys in my rooming house, Randy Schenkat, knew of an opening in his home town, Baraboo, and it wasn't long before I had the job.

Baraboo was a revelation. With its classic town square, rich surrounding farm land, and pristine Devils Lake, it gave me little reason to want to return to the burgeoning strip malls and sand and gravel pits of Southern Maryland. I rented a decent 2 room apartment in the old Philbrick house overlooking the Baraboo River, and began the roller coaster ride of a first year school teacher.

On the first of June, in order to avoid Philbrick's $85 per month rent, I put all my belongings in the trunk of my Dodge Dart and spent the summer living on Lake Wisconsin on an old pontoon boat owned by fellow teacher Chuck Gunderson. There I started each morning with a swim across the Wisconsin River and back.

My social life, however, had become much less strenuous. About the third week in June I decided to take an afternoon drive into Madison, where I pleased myself to think I might still get a warm welcome at the pier behind the Elizabeth Waters dormitory.

But as I drove on Highway 19 just east of the only Waunakee in the World, I looked out over a huge hay field to the North and glimpsed that prototypical Wisconsin summer scene: a tractor, baler, and haywagon crawling up and down windrows as big as rain barrels, packaging the summer harvest in uniform, rectangular, twine-tied, backbreaking bales. An unaccountable impulse made me pull over, get out of the car, and make my way through a barbed wire fence into the field.

Wearing yellow plaid bermuda shorts and black Converse tennis shoes, I jumped on the moving hayrack and asked the hired hand if he could use some help. By evening my hands were bloody and my legs pock-marked from the prickly first crop hay stems. My neck was kinked from being hit in the head with bales falling off the long elevator into the barn mow. This had to be the hardest physical work I had ever done. And in some strange way I felt I had found my calling in life. My next move would be to try to find a farm.

One of my key advisors in this search was Skinny Wallen, a semi-retired clothing salesman who peddled the Botany 500 line at Hoppe Clothing in the morning, and did as he pleased after dinner. Kindred spirits, enchanted by brown cows and hidden valleys, Wallen and I would comb the countryside as far west as Lime Ridge and Ironton looking for Shangri-la. Well-versed in country matters, Skinny would comment on the condition of the fences, the location of the spring, and elicit from the poor farmer and his wife reasons which compelled the sale of the farm.

Though we stumbled on some vistas of heartbreaking beauty (and undeniable poverty), I was afraid that the most alluring available properties were beyond wintertime driving range of Baraboo High School, where I had signed on to teach a second year. I was not naive enough to think I was ready to make a living off of 80 acres of ridge and valley in western Sauk County.

My break came the following summer. A farm only 3 miles west of town was listed in the Classified Section of the Baraboo News Republic—no realtor was involved. Well off the beaten path, the farm was not easy to locate. Finally I found my way down a deadend road, into a deep hollow, across a creek, and up a steep wooded bank to the old Wilhelm place. Burdock and ragweed stood a full six feet high around the unpainted outbuildings, and some 40 pound feeder pigs were rooting in what was left of the back yard.

Old man Wilhelm and neighbor Gordon Martin were coming out the door after a late noon hour as I arrived, and I followed them to the field for an afternoon of haying. The upland meadows over-looking ripening oats and tassling corn were breathtaking; I quickly discounted the unkempt dooryard and crude assortment of hog shanties littering the premises as items not sufficient to negate the farm's scenic beauty and productive potential.

As for my estimation of the farmhouse, I am reminded of Minnesota man Elmer Hansen's report to his bride following his search for a farm in Richland County, Wisconsin. He brought her the news that he had found a gently rolling place with heavy soil much to his liking, and, equally important, affordable. The silo was in good repair and the barn had lever stanchions. When the good woman anxiously asked about the condition of the dwelling, he replied that though the roof was in dire need of shingling, the house appeared to be livable. But further questioning about the kitchen, parlor, running water, etc. forced him to admit he had not taken the time to tour the humble abode. Indeed, his only view of the interior was a quick glimpse of the sagging summer kitchen through a hole in the back door. This lack of domestic inspection had not, however, prevented him from making a down payment and signing a land contract. This way they both could cross the threshold of their new homestead for the first time, sight unseen, for better or for worse.

The year was 1968. Milk plants were threatening to shut off farms which did not replace milk cans with a refrigerated tank for bulk transport. Wilhelm was 62—social security age. His wife had cancer. They had done things the hard way for too many years— plowing with horses, cleaning barn by hand, without children or hired help. They had had enough. They wanted to keep a few acres on top of the hill and put up their dream home—a double wide trailer house. Their asking price: an affordable $19,000. If the truth be known, I was their only serious prospect, and the $19,000 would barely cover the cost of the double wide.

I put up the $3,000 I had saved from two years teaching school, and borrowed the rest. It was a serious step lightly taken. I had never milked a cow, or driven a tractor. I did not know a heifer from a Hereford. There were plenty of backaches and heartaches to come, I knew. But at the age of 25, I owned a farm in Wisconsin. I was home.

"I wanted to look without flinching,
Stand with both feet on the ground,
Make the hard choices for reasons
Fundamentally sound."

POEMS

"He writes not whose poetry nobody reads."

Marcus Martialis

Mike O'Connell and Gordon Martin

"While memory still serves us, we still try
To keep alive our little noon hour lie."

I. HOLE IN MY BUCKET

There's a hole in my bucket, dear Liza, dear Liza,
There's a hole in my bucket, dear Liza, a hole.

Pennsylvania Dutch Folk Song

GOOD INTENTIONS

"If we had world enough, and time." I remember stopping over to see my neighbor, Gordon Martin, one New Year's Eve morning. He was going in several directions trying to take care of unfinished business. The temperature was about 5 degrees and there was a foot of snow on the ground. "There's so much I want to do," he said, "before winter."

I wanted to look without flinching,
Stand with both feet on the ground,
Make the hard choices for reasons
Fundamentally sound.

But my studies were short and sporadic,
My training was brief and veneer,
I started with youth and potential
That gave way to folly and fear.

I wanted to finish the season,
Follow the harvest with plow,
Refill and topfill the silo,
Stack to the peak of the mow.

But November came under the weather,
I'm left with my "ifs" and my "buts,"
And every day would be Christmas
If wishes were candy and nuts.

THE COW THEY COULDN'T KILL

The Dairy Diversion program in the early 1980's was a Congressional effort to reduce the supposed surplus of dairy products. Participating dairy farmers were paid—from heavy milk check deductions from non-participants—to reduce their herd size and annual milk production. Those applying for the program had to verify that they had actually sold some cows and that these cows had gone for slaughter, and not to their neighbor's barn.

Following its 1984 publication in a state farm newspaper, I was told that this poem appeared on bulletin boards at livestock auction barns around Wisconsin, in part due to its mention of the notorious cattle jockey Eldor Buelow.

November 8 the Dairy Bill
Was on the major Network News:
Ten dollars for each hundredweight
You say you won't produce.

I culled two cows November 10,
Two more before December's snow,
But still the bulk tank was too full—
One more would have to go.

This was no time for sentiment,
The D.H.I. sheet[1] told it all:
A "C" for milk, a "D" for fat?
The axe would have to fall.

It didn't take me long to find
The cow who had the lowest score—
The last cow I would ever want
To see go out the door.

[1]The Dairy Herd Improvement Association computerized herd production statistics.

Cows could come and cows could go
But Brandy was my favorite.
She had three daughters milking strong
And she was Red and White.

The slender neck, the sloping rib,
She moved and milked so easily,
Very dairy in the head
And in the mammary.

The trucker said "My God! That cow's
Too good to send to Equity!"
And as she climbed the loading chute
She turned and looked at me.

I'm in the program now, I thought,
These tears won't last another day.
But what a cow to have to sell!
And what a price to pay!

My tears returned on Wednesday noon:
I tore the envelope and found
That Brandy, lovely Brandy, sold
For thirty cents a pound!

Come January it was time
To register with A.S.C.[2]
To show I'd culled some cows and find
Just what my base would be.

The stranger said the rules were tough
And every farmer must adhere,
Then looked at my receipts and said
"We have a problem here."

[2]Agricultural Stabilization and Conservation Service

continued on next page

"This cow you sold the 29th,
The one you say you sent for kill—
Well . . . she didn't get to Green Bay,
And I doubt she ever will.

"As for the Dairy Program, son,
You can forget about it now,
For Mr. Eldor Buelow bought
Your old Red Holstein cow."

The farmers in the office there
All stopped and craned their necks to see
Whose cow it was that found her way
To Eldor's menagerie.

And it may be that some of them
Will never fully understand
Why I reached across the countertop
And shook a stranger's hand.

My cows are free to fill the tank,
Reagan can't put me in jail,
And I can buy my Brandy back
At Eldor's Spring dispersal sale.

HUSBANDMAN

"Friendly persuasion always wins the day
In working with the Holstein dairy cow.
Prod and shackles won't improve your profits—
She gives more milk when treated like a lady."
So I told the local Cloverbuds
In preparation for their dairy projects.

Next morning I was wakened by sharp thunder,
Then pouring rain as I traversed the pasture
To bring the cows in for their morning milking.
On days like this there has to be one straggler,
A cow who'd sooner take a summer drenching
Than stick her neck once more into a stanchion.
I drove her up the hill into the barnyard
Where she decided yond box elder tree
Would make us both a suitable umbrella
And led me underneath its dripping branches.
My shirt was soaked, my shoes were underwater.
I yanked a loose board from the barnyard fence
And whacked her one across her bony rump,
Breaking the board but not her stubbornness.
I kinked her tail in three or four directions,
Called her names from back before the Bible,
Cursed the sorry bull that had conceived her,
And swore that I would send her to McDonald's
Before the sun would go down on my anger;
And as I chewed her out, she chewed her cud.
Just then a voice called gently from the doorway:
"Come pretty Bossy, see what's here for breakfast."
With that the critter left me in the quagmire
And sauntered to the barn for grain and silage.
The door was quickly shut and barred behind her—
I had to make my entry through a hay chute.

continued on next page

A half hour later came her turn for milking:
She drew her head up from her morning ration,
Turned back her neck inside the yoke to see
If I was wielding any deadly weapon.
I called her name and set up close beside her,
Stroked her knobby tailhead with my fingers,
Buried my head into her well-rinsed flank,
And braced myself for her retaliation.
She could have sent me sprawling in the gutter,
Or peeled a shard off from her master's shoulder.
But she stood still as if nothing had happened—
It was not in her docile bovine nature,
This foster mother of the human race,
To act as if two wrongs could make a right.

I spent some extra time washing her udder
And slid the milker on so gently that
She had to know that all had been forgiven
And I would henceforth treat her like a lady—
The lady of the house would see to that.

OFF-FARM INCOME

One of the key recommendations of the University's "Center For Dairy Profitability" was that farmers find ways to supplement shrinking milk checks with off-farm employment. Economically, this was little more than robbing Peter to pay Paul, and too often it accelerated the demise of rural family life.

The spare, two-beat lines of "Off-Farm Income" echo Frost's "The Hill Wife," but the stronger influence may be the much-admired verse of Stephen Vincent Benet. When my high school students were required to memorize a poem for recitation, Benet's brief and touching "Nancy Hanks" was a popular choice.

Times were lean
And the milk price down
So she took to part time
Waitress in town.

Leaving him
And the boy to farm.
Well after dark
They'd come in from the barn

To a silent supper
And wait 'til she came.
And who am I
To say who's to blame

But one night she didn't
Come home by ten,
And they went to bed
Wondering when.

She was home by the time
They woke to chore,
And she never blinked,
And he never swore,

continued on next page

But *something* had happened,
Something had broke,
And you'd have to know
About country folk

To know it was over
Deep inside
And the three of them suffered
Until they died.

SONG OF THE WEARY FARMER

Mama said there'd be days like this—she just never said there'd be so many in a row.

My bucket's got a hole in it,
Just don't have my heart and soul in it,
Can't remember any goal in it—
I ain't gonna milk no more.

Country Times says there's such fun in it,
Not when there ain't any mon in it,
Sure don't ever want my son in it—
I ain't gonna milk no more.

Evenin' sky has got some rain in it,
Cows are sloshin' down the lane in it,
O my back has got a pain in it—
I ain't gonna milk no more.

Was a time I put some pep in it,
Only God knows why I kep' in it,
Watch yourself so you don't step in it—
Stand back and let me milk once more.

BARNS OF WISCONSIN

In the 1980's the State Department of Agriculture used the term "retirement" as a euphemism for "foreclosure" in the farm community.

The Division of Tourism lost no sleep over displaced farm families, but there was deep concern over the tarnished image of Wisconsin Dairying. Committees were formed around the state to spruce up vacant and deteriorating barns, in order to preserve our heritage and provide pleasant windshield scenery for the good people of Illinois.

Our cows are at the packing plant,
Our heifers in New Mexico,
But let there be no weeping in
The dairy afterglow.

Burdock claims the barnyard now,
The bankrupt farmer's gone to town,
But God forbid the dairy barn
Should ever tumble down.

Call the Sherwin-Williams store
To keep the home place looking quaint,
And give that weather-beaten barn
A hot red coat of paint.

Plant pansies round the milkhouse door
For all the cockeyed world to see,
And never let the tourists know
Wisconsin's tragedy.

A shadow falls upon the land,
But do not falter, do not grieve,
We must keep our chins up in
Our land of make believe.

HE KNEW WHERE HE WAS HEADED

Coming out of the movie theatre one night in the early 1980's, a friend could not help but notice that I had been much moved by the plight of the farm family in Country, *starring Jessica Lange.*

"But that was in Iowa," she said.

Before the end of the decade the farm crisis had a chokehold on Wisconsin as well. Some quit, some foreclosed, some refinanced, some expanded. Some broke down; some cracked up. Some hung on for dear life. And some went looking for a gun, or a rope, or a ladder.

When feed was short, and times were lean,
Little was there to cheer,
And farmers round the township sighed
"This could be my last year."

But Tommy Tate was undeterred.
To quit would be disgrace:
"They'll have to grab my arms and legs
And drag me off the place."

To show he was in earnest
To farm for the long haul,
He bought a silo, steel and glass,
And eighty-eight feet tall.

Got married to a country girl,
Began a family—
The sky would be the limit
As far as we could see.

But those who we are passing by
While rising to renown
May be the same ones we will meet
When we come crashing down.

continued on next page

One night Tom climbed the Harvestore,
Stood up against the stars,
Cursed the old man in the moon,
And flipped the bird at Mars.

He saw the swingset in the yard,
He saw the lights of town,
He saw the moonlit pavement
Eighty-eight feet down.

They missed him in the morning
With bunks and mangers bare,
While hungry calves were calling
A man who wasn't there.

Blame it on the milk price,
Blame it on the drought,
Blame the silo salesman
Who tapped poor Tommy out.

Tom saw his ending early on,
There was no saving face,
They took hold of his arms and legs,
And dragged him off the place.

AT THE SAUK COUNTY
UNEMPLOYMENT OFFICE

Following the floods of 1993—we had 13 inches of rain in three hours one Saturday night in July—various farmers' assistance programs were formulated by State and Federal agencies. To apply for compensation, farmers were obliged to stand in line at their local unemployment office.

We had survived the flood. The question was how to survive another year of milk prices below the cost of production.

The building is new and spacious,
With a two-tiered parking lot.
The government is investing heavily
In this growth industry.

Farmers in an unemployment line?
"I didn't want to come,"
We tell each other,
Blaming our presence on the proddings
Of the wife, the minister . . .

Look in the book under "work ethic"
You should see a picture of these men:
Descendants of immigrants, pioneers, homesteaders,
Giants of the earth . . .
Men who made their way
Using good and bad luck
Like they used their two hands
Now lining up for crumbs from Uncle Sam.

This is not the destitution
Of the Great Depression.
We have all had our breakfast.
The woodpile will carry us until Spring.

continued on next page

For some there are "assets" left to liquidate
Before they take our farms away.
Five miles up the road
They are hiring blackjack dealers
At the Ho Chunk casino.

Yet we are living proof
That "living off the land"
Is no longer any kind of living.
Those who fill the nation's breadbasket
With "cheap food"
Cannot put groceries on the table,
Much less pay the taxes on the land.
The milk cow who must support
The processors, the dairy boards,
The P.R. agencies, the USDA superfunds,
Has nothing left to give the hands that feed her.

"Relief" for farmers?
Relief will come
Only with revolution.

HERMITAGE

Not uncommon among even the more gregarious and openhearted of the Irish is a corresponding need for seclusion, reflection, secrecy. As Bob Cummings of Rt. 4 Baraboo once said, "A man ought to have a little business no one else knows anything about."

No visible means of support,
No job that the neighbors can see,
Some heifers mowing the dooryard
And a gnarly crabapple tree.

It's been a long time since the phone rang,
But I know when to go for the mail;
I keep track of the wind and the weather,
I measure the rain in a pail.

It's just about all I can handle,
Containing my destiny:
I husband my storehouse of silence,
My shelf of obscurity.

AFTER DINNER

*I once asked a well-mechanized farmer how things were working out
since his wife took a town job. He professed to like the new arrangement.
"This way," he said, "I don't have to stop for dinner."*

To each his own.

The neighbor rings my telephone to say
He'll slip over after dinner with a rack
If I can help him stack a load of hay.
His "after dinner" always takes me back
To times when dinner crowned the working day,
And noon hour meant what it's supposed to mean:
An hour for rest, and nourishment, and play.
Hot food and banter filled the kitchen scene
Until we turned, renewed, to tasks at hand
In field or wood . . . the platters cracked and cold,
Only his words resound to grace the land—
Some tang of those times he would have us hold.

While memory still serves us, we still try
To keep alive our little noon hour lie.

GOOD NIGHT

Sleepless with sciatica during the winter of 1993-94, I found some diversion, if not relief, in nightly walks of two or three miles. A poor man's cure, I was told, was to simply "walk it off." Even at below-zero temperatures, I gave it my best shot, picking up the pace as the pain got worse.

So I am not the only ancient man
Pursuing life like some deranged dragoon:
At midnight in the February sky
I see Orion reaching for the moon.

FARMER OF THE YEAR

Farmers heralded by University types for their risk-taking expansion ventures and adoption of state of the art technology often skate on very thin ice. Some fifteen years ago I was at an open house for a newly-installed carousel milking parlor south of Loganville. I inquired as to the whereabouts of the owner. The word was that he had to be in town that day to complete papers for foreclosure on his farm.

Wisconsin's Dairy Breeders
With members far and near
Named a Muenster County man
Their Farmer of the Year.

An editor who knew me well
Said "Take a half a day
And bring us back a full report
From over Withee Way."

I finished all my chores by noon
Then put my truck in gear
And hit the open road to find
The Farmer of the Year.

As I pulled into Withee town
The streets and stores were still.
A sign down by the river read
"Moriarity's Mill."

A farmer backed up to the stove
Said "You're a stranger here."
I said "I've come to interview
The Farmer of the Year."

A half a dozen heads looked up
And then somebody swore.
I said "I need to find the farm
Of Linus Lattimore."

At this the tongues were loosened
And I was forced to hear
The latest local gossip on
The Farmer of the Year.

"I'd tell you how to find the place
But Linus won't be there,
He's at a big convention—
Best Western—in Eau Claire.

"He'll be back Monday afternoon
In time to hear the scoop
That his crackerjack hired man
Has up and flown the coop.

"Now we'll see if Liney boy
Knows how to drop a plow
Or how to put a milker on
A temperamental cow.

"You might find his poor son-in-law
Between his trips to town
For parts for their blue Harvestore
That's always breaking down.

"Drove past the place last Saturday,
I'm glad I didn't stop.
The soup in their big slurrystore
Was running over top.

"His wife works at the Courthouse now,
No flies on her fur coat,
She learned to like the lights of town
And that was all she wrote."

continued on next page

I said "You boys have said enough,
My ears are getting sore."
But still one codger hailed me
As I headed for the door.

"If there's a Hell for fancy farmers,
That's where Linus will be sent:
He owes me for a load of hay
And two years' pasture rent."

I pray to God for cows that milk
And corn that fills the ear,
But spare me that cruel title of
The Farmer of the Year.

FROST AS FARMER

There is much to admire in the wisdom of Robert Frost's poetry, much to envy in his sustained popularity, much to question in his cunning and deception.

"The young Frost did a considerable amount of farming . . . he knew something about living off the land . . . by the time he died, he had owned . . . four farms in New Hampshire and Vermont."

Joseph Brodsky, *The New Yorker*, Sept. 26, 1994.

He knew the names of things.
He might have tapped a maple tree,
Chopped wood, picked apples,
Done a little gardening,
Stopped by woods on a savvy evening.
As for the farming part—
Crafty Yankee living off the land—
I won't buy that.
His land was handed him
By a wealthy grandfather,
He harvested one-liners
From neighbors he looked down on,
Taught school to pay the taxes,
Left unpaid debts behind him,
Was gone to England
Before he was forty.

When he came home to fame
North of Boston won him sinecure:
For his last forty years
He slept in featherbeds
At fashionable colleges

continued on next page

Where he could go onstage
In rumpled suit
And thatched white hair
And play the part
Of one who'd just come in
From out of doors
Toting his pail of chestnuts.

II. UNIVERSITY TRIALS

Representative J.S. Williams (Mississippi): "Mr. Hoard, isn't oleomargarine a wholesome and healthful product?"

W.D. Hoard: "No, not as compared with butter."

Williams: "Don't all the chemists here declare that it is?"

Hoard: "Chemists, like certain lawyers, can be got to advocate most anything for the money."

Williams: "Do you mean to say these scientific gentlemen have no honor in what they say on the question?"

Hoard: "Mr. Williams, I mean to say that certain chemists are the scientific prostitutes of the day and age."

Congressional Record

PUTTING IN THE SEED

A new economic and ecological strategy brought forth in the 1980's was L.I.S.A.—low-input, sustainable agriculture. If farmers could do little or nothing about falling commodity prices, they might improve their bottom line by intelligently reducing inputs. Instead of aiming to get rich, farmers should try to keep from going broke. Instead of trying to win prizes growing 200 bushel corn, farmers should focus on profit per acre and conservation of resources.

If the truth be known, however, Grandpa had farmed this way all his life. He called it "keeping the overhead down."

On cold winter evenings
He liked to read reports
Of new alfalfa varieties
Yielding 120% of Vernal
In University trials—
Multileafed, disease resistant,
Superfast recovery,
Ideal for direct seeding
Following an application of Eptam.[1]
He studied the "improved" oats varieties,
Wisconsin Certified Blue Ribbon,
High-proteined, rust-proof, stiff-strawed.
He looked at ads for heavy iron
For no-till, ridge-till, chisel-till,
Low interest while they last.

Then on Good Friday
He cracked open the door
Of the old, dry granary,
Took a handful of oats
Whose name he did not remember,

continued on next page

---

[1]A potent chemical herbicide.

Counted 100 kernels on a wet cloth,
Folded the cloth over,
Wrapped it around a corn cob,
And stuck it in a Mason jar.

In a few days,
After the plump seeds sent
White tendrils knifing through the cotton,
And after a southwest breeze
Had dried the mellowed surface
Of the fall-plowed furrows,
He hitched an old tractor
To an even older disk,
And lightly touched the field.

Then he filled the grain boxes
Of the wooden-wheeled Van Brunt drill
With his 98% germination granary oats
And into the grass seed hopper
Poured a pail of medium red clover
From a bag that was his door prize
From Seed Days at the Mill.

See him on his way
Leading a chorus of blackbirds,
Covering chains jangling
As he circles the field,
Knowing, as sure as Death,
That no God or Devil,
Chemical or weevil,
Can thwart the emergence
Of his emerald stand.

ALL HAIL TO MONSANTO

(Arranged by the UW-Extension Choir)

The deep pockets of the chemical companies allowed them to buy influence for approval of Bovine Growth Hormone injections in State Legislatures and at the Food and Drug Administration. More discouraging was the way they were able to silence any dissent from within Land Grant Universities, institutions founded to preserve, protect, and defend family farms.

BGH had no redeeming social or economic value for farmers, cows, or consumers. But the prospect of a $26 million Biotech Center on the University of Wisconsin-Madison campus was enough to guarantee undivided support from career-conscious faculty and extension agents.

Mammon will not be denied,
Science must not taste defeat.
Principle must step aside—
Stand back and let the Big Dog eat.

Do not rile the Juggernaut,
Kneel and worship at his feet.
Who can know what God hath wrought?
Stand back and let the Big Dog eat.

Ours is not to reason why,
Let us make our meek retreat.
We must submit or we must die—
Stand back and let the Big Dog eat.

WHITE MAN'S BURDEN

The story in "White Man's Burden" is apocryphal. It is true that Bob Pate once donated a tractor to a South American goodwill expedition. It is also true that he saved some of his choicest expletives for the University of Wisconsin College of Agriculture.

As farm foreclosures decimate Wisconsin,
Our farm advisors like to take vacation.
One time some state officials organized
A delegation to Bolivia
To share the secrets of our nonsuccess
With some Latinos north of Capricorn.

Before departure it occurred to one
Just recently pried from his swivel chair
To take some hardware on this pilgrimage
To teach the new religion of hi-tech.
Equipment dealers in surrounding counties
Were asked what could they donate to the cause?

Pate met the U. boys coming in the door.
"You mean since I can't sell a tractor local,
I'd send one on your Good Ship Lollipop?"
He turned them back towards Madtown in a hurry,
Then hollered as they hustled towards the highway,
"I'll have one ready for you Monday morning!"

"Which one you gonna let 'em borrow, Bob?"
Came from a cracker barrel in the corner.
"You think that they could crank up our old Cockshutt?"
Bob looked out the window at his lineup,
Then barked his order at the chief mechanic:
"Bring up that one just in from Osseo;
We'll run 'er through the shop for Bucky Badger."
(The laughter rattled big bolts in the parts bin.)

An ancient Minny was pulled front and center,
Its yellow color now more rust than paint.
The block was cracked, the steering wheel was missing,
The flat rear tires were neither on nor off,
The radiator and the oil pan—dry.
"Take off the drawbar and the generator,
And any other parts that we can salvage,
And point this baby towards Bolivia."

The technocrats arrived before the cargo,
In time to brace the natives for the shock
Of U.S. labor-saving gadgetry.
The peasants stared in awe as Robert's Minny
Rolled down some planks and skidded to a stop
In a barren field next to San Borja school.
They tried to fathom how this iron monster
Could break the hardpan on the Altipano
Or help to speed the harvest of the Coca.
The gringos groped for any explanation:
"We'll wait until the manual arrives
Before we put this one in operation."

Just then the little school let loose for recess.
Brown children ran to see the U.F.O.
Dropped on their playground by an alien people.

Today the children's children share the scene.
They climb and play upon the strange machine.
Praise God for Minneapolis-Moline.

AGAINST THE GRAIN

The fictional Riley represents a long tradition of contrary Wisconsin dairy farmers. His conserving, close to the vest farming practices in the face of conventional scientific wisdom not only set him apart, but make him successful.

"The University is not here for the exceptional man."

Professor Felix Schelling
University of Pennsylvania

The University would tell you how to farm,
And maybe it won't do you too much harm
To listen to what experts have to say—
But Riley always did it Riley's way.

The book says "Plant that corn the first of May!"
For Riley it was Decoration Day.
"Vernal is the worst seed you can buy!"
Riley's stands were thick, and three feet high.

"Throw that Farmer's Almanac away!
Knock that hay down every thirty days!
Be aggressive, nip it in the bud!
Start chopping it at midnight in the mud!"

Riley cut in June, and August too,
Cut clover only when the west wind blew;
When it rained, he took it all in stride,
Filled the barn and stacked the rest outside.

"Cull anything that won't give 60 pounds!"
But Riley kept those two year olds around,
Combed their tails, and whispered in their ear,
And bred them back to milk another year.

"Feed bone meal, blood meal, shoot some BST!"
Riley fed them what he got for free—
No chance of that fourth stomach out of whack
When bossy chews on timothy and quack.

"Crunch numbers, let computers do the work!"
There's Riley outside sharpening his fork.
He checks the pasture from his tractor seat—
I think he's caught another cow in heat.

"Forty cows? You'll never stay alive!"
Riley keeps no more than twenty-five.
"Expand and borrow while the rates are down!"
Riley carries money into town.

The truth be told, there never was a time
When I could match old Riley in his prime,
And yet he taught me there's a lot to gain
From knowing when to go against the grain.

DAIRY SCIENCE CHRISTMAS

After a decade of buying influence in high places, Monsanto finally gained FDA approval of its synthetic bovine growth hormone product, Posilac, just before the holidays in 1993. By this time some of the Monsanto researchers had taken posts inside the FDA, where they could pretend to be objective reviewers of their own company's data.

God rest ye merry dairymen, let nothing you dismay.
You must accept this biotech, there is no other way.
A shot on Christmas Eve could mean more milk on Christmas Day.
O tidings of comfort and joy, comfort and joy,
O tidings of comfort and joy.

Now there will be some suffering, your finest cow may fall,
But you must keep the needle sharp, your back's against the wall.
Don't skip a single stanchion and don't miss a single stall.
O tidings of comfort and joy, comfort and joy,
O tidings of comfort and joy.

Before you go to church today, or after you come back,
Give your cows their Christmas gift, the gift of Posilac,
And pray to God that somehow you will get your money back.
O tidings of comfort and joy, comfort and joy,
O tidings of comfort and joy.

Tonight there lies a baby in a manger far away.
He might not like to see the things we do to cows today.
But he still has his eyes closed—ssshh!—don't wake him right away.
O tidings of comfort and joy, comfort and joy,
O tidings of comfort and joy.

III. IN THE FIELD

And year by year she has betrayed him
With blight and mildew, rain and drought,
Smut, scab, and murrain, all the rout;
But he forgets the tricks she's played him
   When first
The fields give a good smell and the leaves put me out.

Aye, come the Spring, and the gulls keening,
Over her strumpet lap he'll ride,
Watching those wasteful fields and wide,
Where the darkened tilth will soon be greening,
   With looks
Fond and severe, as looks the groom on bride.

a wife's lament from "The Rival"

SOWING OATS:
SEEDS OF MEMORY

I crank them through the fanning mill,
Then pour the plumpest in the drill,
And as I sow beyond the lea
I never lack for company.

The blackbirds sing, the sea gulls swoop,
The chickens fly the chicken coop
To follow where the furrows lead
And check the quality of seed.

No need to fly into a rage—
I stop to check the bushel gauge
And nudge the dial from three to four
To widen every hopper door.

One to peck and three to thrash
Hardly keeps me long on cash,
But fowl make sure I'm not the fool
Who sows a stand too thick to stool.

CONFESSION

The great critic Randall Jarrell wrote that "a good poet is someone who manages, in a lifetime of standing out in thunderstorms, to be struck by lightning five or six times."

Yet poetry is not only nor always the result of electric moments of epiphany. It may also depend on careful and ceaseless word-crafting, the rational, deliberate building of sound and sense into unforgettable lines. What writer does not envy the conscious fusion of the casual and the majestic in the couplets of A.E. Housman's "To An Athlete Dying Young":
> *Runners whom renown outran*
> *And the name died before the man.*

I never felt the visionary rage
That wrenches self-expression to the page.
I've had some joys, some sorrows in my time—
No need to box them into stifled rhyme.

This is not to say verse sickens me—
I rummage in old books of poetry
Some rainy days, and hunt a line or so
To ponder on, or maybe keep for show,

But sunshine turns the schoolboy out to play,
To vernal field, or summer holiday . . .
Life's studded moments, oh so quick to flee,
Why pluck into Art's pale eternity?

. . . Yet what I'd give to turn a line or so
Some callow youth would like to keep for show.

DON'T LOOK NOW

I have long been enchanted by the sweet sadness of Ernest Dowson's brief lyric entitled "Envoy," which contains the line "They are not long, the days of wine and roses."

In "Don't Look Now" I have borrowed Dowson's simple but unusual verse pattern, in which the surprisingly short final line seems a reminder of our mortality.

> **"None of them knew the color of the sky."**
>
> Stephen Crane

The fields are rife with corn and beans and clover,
Yellow, bronze, and green,
Wild sumac fires the fringes of October's
Splendid scene.

But days are short, and winter is eternal,
To gaze would be a sin
Before each bale is in the mow, each kernel
In the bin.

HELP WANTED

In the spring of 1994 I was a displaced farmer with a bad back. I looked for employment as a teacher, coach, reporter, surveyor, editor, laborer, only to find I had become persona non grata among employers. What I had worked at or accomplished in my life before milking cows meant nothing.

One of the pleasures I could always take in reading Death of a Salesman *was that I knew my problems were not as great as Willy's. Now the distance between us was narrowing fast.*

A factory job I was denied—
They called me overqualified;
An office job would pay some bills
But I had no computer skills.

Too old for this, too weak for that,
I had no place to hang my hat,
So even though the season's short
The orchard was my last resort.

No need to send a resumé—
They hire whoever comes their way:
Mel is lame, Jack is quick,
They only pay for what you pick.

No card to punch, no clock to watch,
A dollar for each level box.
Here's your ladder, there's your tree:
It's equal opportunity.

APPLEJACK

During the 1994 harvest season at Maple Hill Orchard I was amazed at both the bounty of the crop and the vast amount of fruit which never made it to the shed, much less to the table.

The heavy Cortlands like to fall,
My fingers cannot catch them all.
For every three my hand goes round
A fourth escapes, and hits the ground.

So on this pippin perfect day
I know what made the poet say:
"What wondrous life is this I lead:
Ripe apples drop about my head."

I know what Isaac Newton knew:
An apple falls when it is due,
Obeys the law of gravity,
And never falls far from the tree.

The ones below will bear a bruise
Which bars them from commercial use:
Unfit for basket or for pie,
The apple pickers let them lie.

We have more apples than we need,
Yet it is not an act of greed
When I return at dusk to sack
The underlings for applejack.

You take the seamless, rosy fruit
And sell it to whom it may suit;
Leave me the windfalls in the grass—
I like them golden in a glass.

TRUE LIES

Our apple picking crew in the fall of 1994 included a democratic assortment of characters, most of them down on their luck: a few broken down dairy farmers, an unemployed civil engineer, a knock-off man from the foundry, some daytrippers from the Huber Center, a pair of young lovers, and Ted McCracken, who put us all in the shade.

We had a cowboy in our orchard crew,
A bandy-legged, story-telling outlaw.
His skin was chafed by sun and rope and leather—
His hair gone, his hat full of feathers.

While we picked Cortlands, Ted talked picking cotton.
He'd travelled all the Rocky Mountain region,
Cooked at a dude ranch west of Laramie,
Thrashed grain from Abilene to North Dakota,
Drove at a hundred twenty miles an hour
From San Antonio to Dallas—naked—
With some señorita from Laredo.
Such were the stories we were forced to swallow
As we picked our way up the pointed ladders
Out of earshot of the storyteller.
The rest of us had never left Wisconsin—
Whatever we had done, Ted had done better;
Whatever we had seen, Ted had seen wilder.
There wasn't any place that you could mention
From West Virginia to New Mexico
But Ted had been there, likely even *lived* there.
He was a legend in his day and mind.
And yet there was a time that Ted said something
That wasn't any kind of boast or lie
And we still wonder at the reason why.

That morning we were sizing up the trees,
Staking claims and stacking empty boxes
Along a row of heavy Macintosh,
Each sagging with the weight of twenty bushel.
And yet between two of the loaded trees
Almost unnoticed in September mist
Stood one bereft of yellow, red, or green,
A gnarled skeleton of sticks
Supported by a twisted, cloven trunk
Hid among some thick Canada thistle—
Its only harvest now would be with chainsaw.
We made whatever jokes that came to mind
About this death-in-life or life-in-death
And someone said "Who's going to pick old Bones?"
Ted was not jesting when he turned to me:
"You know that cripple looks a lot like me."

Since when did Ted do business with the facts?
Or make himself seem less than Wyatt Earp?
Or could it be that we had been mistaken
In writing off his tales as cock and bull?
Could he have really killed that man in Tulsa?
Fathered a son by a Shoshone princess?
Had Teddy's legend been too strange for fiction?
Or was it just that, getting long in tooth,
He thought it time for coming home to truth?

LOST IN RICHLAND COUNTY

High upon a rolling ridge today a
Lonesome valley hurt my eye the way a
Song can make you cry and want to play a
Nother mountain side of Kathy Mattea.

PALE FIRE

I wrote this poem on a Sunday night, as a kind of counterpoint to "How Great Thou Art," which we had sung in church that morning.

I watched the sun on Easter rise
Like it was just another day.
When summer lightning split the skies
I had no call to kneel and pray.

The perfect pitch of Autumn's choir,
The tremble of each hardwood leaf,
Could not set my soul on fire
Nor shake me into true belief.

But I heard the voice of Jesus cry
In a tired old Laredo tune;
I saw God through a buttermilk sky
On a bare November afternoon.

END OF NOVEMBER

There are many arguments for deer hunting in Wisconsin. We need to "harvest" deer which might otherwise not survive the winter. Excessive deer numbers lead to crop losses for farmers. Deer licenses bring in needed revenue for the Department of Natural Resources. Hunting provides "good clean fun" in the "great outdoors" for thousands of red-blooded sportsmen.

The opinions of the deer have gone unrecorded.

No truck nor tourist knows their deadend lane,
And yet upon returning late from town
The wife lets off the gas and shifts her down
To walking speed—he asks her to explain.

"Allen walks his dog long after dark,
And what if Gordon's coming round the bend,
No headlights on his tractor once again?
We're almost there—did you hear Mandy bark?"

And then it happens—her *true* fear:
Crossing the roadway, blinded by the light,
High-stepping foursome in nocturnal flight—
A graceful, fearful family of deer.

Safe beyond the ditch, before they go,
They look back from a clearing at the car,
Amazed at cheating death, yet still so far
From being out of the woods, for they well know

The brake has saved the night, but who's to say
The blaze of dawn won't bring a crueller fate?
Buckshot and bullet will fly swift and straight;
The creek will run red for the holiday.

BEYOND CONFUSION
FOR DORIS BRECKA

While traffic jams the highway
Hellbent for God knows where,
I know a hidden valley
Well off the thoroughfare.

Change and innovation
May spin the world around,
Yet there's a greater merit
In holding solid ground.

Let me find a handle,
Let me sink a plow,
Let me carry water
To a chicken or a cow.

Let me know the purpose,
The patience and the power
Of the earthworm in the furrow,
The pistil in the flower.

"Did I not give my son the name
Of one the gods could never tame?"

IV.   ANECDOTES FOR FATHERS

They were ninety years old and of their seventeen children had just buried the first born son who died at seventy-two years of age.

"I told you," said the man as he and his hillborn wife sat on the cabin steps in the evening sunset, "I told you long ago we would never raise that boy."

Carl Sandburg

MONROE, WISCONSIN: SUMMER, 1955

My maternal grandfather and I had a good deal in common—love of sports, fascination with the Civil War, and an unabashed affection for the land and people of Wisconsin. But his views on farming were colored by some apparently harsh memories of nineteenth century backwoods agriculture. Like Abraham Lincoln and Frank Lloyd Wright, he thought farming was a good thing to get out of your system as early as possible. Born in the city, I looked at it as an experience I had been denied as a boy. I was on the outside, looking for a way in.

The town square celebrated in the poem resembles the one in Baraboo, eighty miles north.

After showing me
The might and majesty
Of the Waukesha MotorWorks,
My grandfather,
Farm boy become production manager,
Drove me down to old Monroe—
His brother practiced dentistry
In the County Seat.
(Success was running in the family.)

Rain from the night before
Flooded the noonday scene with
Farm families come to town
To shop and barter.
My head spun to see
Tractors pulling carts filled with
Towheads and grain sacks.

Double tavern doors opened wide,
Spilling smells of beer and limburger
Out into the street
Where sunlight flashed
In puddles by the curb.

continued on next page

Around the market square
Women in checkered kerchiefs
Toted bundles beside
Stout smiling men with hands
The color of the earth

Some had finished haying
Before the storm–others
Had had their windrows rained on.
Who cared? Today was holiday:
Clean overalls and a stick of penny candy
And gossip you could never hear at home.

This was the pungent pageant,
The people and the life
Grandpa had left behind.
What was farming anyway
But pulling tits and forking shit
Day after day, year after year?
He had come up from slavery
And though he tried and tried that day
Could not identify
Among the throng a single face
From the village of his youth.
(We met the dentist briefly in his office.)

Driving home in the gloaming
I could see Guernseys
Heading in from pasture,
Rows of lighted windows
On motley farmsteads.
And if Grandpa had dared
Take his eyes off the road
He might have seen
There in the Studebaker
A frail and freckled city boy
Already rolling up his sleeves,
Looking for a barn to put some cows in.

GENERATIONS OF MEN

In mid-September, 1994, my neighbor, Gordon Martin, was still trying to make first crop hay. Laid up with lumbago, I was in no shape to help him stack or unload bales. But towards sunset one warm evening, the thumping of the baler plunger in a distant field was irresistible. I followed the tractor path to the field, where he was doing his usual double-duty: driving tractor and baler as well as stacking the wagon load behind. I drove the H for him the last few rounds of the day as we watched the sky blacken on the northern horizon. It had been twenty-five years since Gordon first taught me how to stack a load of hay; we were now mere shadows of our former selves. I wrote the entire poem later that evening.

Hamstrung by lumbago, the old farmer,
Relegated to the back porch rocker,
Whittles away the summer afternoon,
Almost asleep, almost asleep for good,
Until the rhythm of the baler plunger
KAROOMPH KAROOMPH KAROOMPH KAROOMPH
    KAROOMPH
In the oval field just west behind the pines
Reverberates more in his heart than ears,
Somehow resuscitates his failing pulse,
And calls him one more time from death to life.
Legs, arms twitch with some forgotten impulse.
He topples off the porch, then finds his footing,
Following the sound of the machinery.
The painful hitch that slows his getalong
Can't keep him from the timeless task at hand.

Coming up the windrow with the baler,
Son and grandson see him at the field's edge,
His sunken eyes near blinded by glaucoma,
Yet crazy with excitement in the sunlight.

continued on next page

"Here's Grandpa come to run the show again.
He thinks he'll stack a load clear up to Heaven,
When he can't even crawl up on the wagon."
Such are the words of the fourteen year old,
As yet untouched by cruel mortality.

The son takes time to idle down the tractor.
"Say pa, you think you could drive tractor for us?
This field is almost more than we can handle."
He lifts the crumpled body to the high seat,
Then sets himself atop a flattopped fender
Where he can help the old man with the steering.

Around the field they crawl beside the windrows,
Grandson stacking bales like young Adonis,
Tireless in the golden glow of youth,
Impatient at the geriatric pace:
"Hey Dad, I've got a ballgame at 6:30—
Why don't you slowpokes open up the throttle?"

But Grandpa's lost in eighty years of haying:
Buck rake, dump rake, stacker, tedder, crimper,
Hauling loose hay to the barn with horses,
Line storm racing with them down the field road.

One little circle of the field completed,
Son brings his father back to terra firma,
And shouts his thanks directly in his ear:
"I know you've got some other work to do,
But thanks for helping tie up a few bales—
Tell Ma we'll stop for supper in an hour."

Grandpa is all smiles at the table
As family review the day's adventures:
"I see it took three men to do the baling,"
Says someone tongue-in-cheek from down the table.
"Well, yes, the windrows seemed so awful heavy,

The radio kept calling for a shower,
And Junior had to make it to a ballgame.
Good thing that Grandpa offered to drive tractor."

Six weeks later came the second cutting,
Son and grandson back on Grandpa's hayfield
Some four days following the funeral.

"You got a game tonight?"

     "No."

      "Well, that's good.

This time around it's just the two of us.
It's going to take us just a little longer
Because . . ." The boy was ready now to listen.

"He must have baled it alone a hundred times.
Ripped it with a horse-drawn quack digger,
Picked rock by moonlight after evening milking,
Sowed clover, brome, and timothy by hand,
Built his haycocks stout against the weather . . .
How would you like to perch on a little stool
Aside a herky jerky antique baler
And hand-tie wire around each bloody bale?"

With that he pulls the power takeoff handle.
The grandson jumps aboard the empty wagon
In jeans and t-shirt and old tennis shoes.
Already in his seventh summer haying,
He pulls his well worn chore gloves from his pockets:
He'll try to stack a load against the ages.

LITTLE LEAGUE

I once coached a baseball team of nine and ten year olds. During the late innings of a close game, with our team at bat, I noticed several of our players in a circle at the far end of the dugout. The object of their interest was a Mason jar filled with muddy water and a few crayfish which the second baseman had brought to the game, perhaps to take his mind off baseball.

I thought about this poem while watching Ken Burns's nine part series, Baseball, *on Public Television in September, 1994. Burns would have you believe every red-blooded boy in America lives for the game. I beg to differ. Baseball is a dangerous, often cruel sport, especially as organized in our Little Leagues.*

Chris is afraid of the coaches,
Billy's afraid of the ball,
Andy's afraid of a third strike,
Whether it's swinging, or called.

Dan is afraid of his daddy,
He plays for a semi pro team,
He hollers from high in the bleachers,
It's hard to let go of his dream.

But the grounders are too hot to handle,
The popups get lost in the sun,
O Lord get us out of the inning,
The damage is already done.

Freddie's been hit by a fastball,
Sam was just spiked in the shin,
The coaches are having a rhubarb
Over which inning we're in.

But what are those clouds on the hilltop?
Was that just thunder I heard?
We could be in for a downpour!
Let's give the umpire the word

To call off the game before lightning
Strikes some aluminum chair,
Lord give the infield a soaking
Down to the nightcrawlers' lair.

Give us a squall on the river,
Bring up the carp in the lake,
Give us a respite from baseball,
For Joey, and Jimmy, and Jake.

Give us some puddles for splashing,
Make us some mud from the clay,
Grant us a glorious raincheck—
Give us some children at play.

FORTY NINE AND NINE

*There is an age when a father cannot help but be a disappointment
to a son.*

When you went to bed last night
You asked if I
Could fix your bicycle chain
And untangle the line
Inside your fishing reel.

Sad to say
I could not find the metric wrenches
And I still have not been able
To declaw the catgut in the reel.

Though you didn't ask me to,
I did manage
To tweak the tension in your hunting bow.

I know, I know.

When you get home from school today
Find your sharpest arrow,
And set an apple on my head.

DAN AND DEN

With Pythias condemned to death
Friend Damon drew a shortened breath;
So Pythias could go on bail,
Damon put himself in jail.
*Said "Kill **me** if he won't return!"*
Whereby Dionysius learned
That love between the young and brave
Cannot be thwarted by the grave.

One at a time, they're not so bad,
My third grade son, and the neighbor lad,
But put them together, they're a pair
To drive a parent to despair
With running, jumping, hullabaloo,
Two wild and crazy kangaroos.

After a terrible afternoon
I send one home, and one to his room,
And hope to die and cross my heart
That I will keep these twerps apart.
How much more can one man stand
Of Dan and Den, of Den and Dan?

Late in the evening, a knock at my door—
"I s'pose I can't see Den no more?"
And later still, amid the gloom,
The stifled sobbing from his room.
No brother there for love and play
And now I take his pal away.

Have I forgotten all the joys
Of healthy, hurly-burly boys?
Did I not give my son the name
Of one the gods could never tame?
Might these two not be, in the end,
Damon—and Pythias—again?

OUT OF THE LOOP

There may be a hundred spurious stories in Sandburg's Life of Lincoln. In time we come to distrust what may be genuine. "Out of the Loop" draws from earlier sources a story both shocking and authentic, one which does not serve to deify nor degrade the man, yet adds still another layer to his mystery.

Although Judge Davis and his circuit-riding lawyers were on the road for weeks at a time, if their immediate venue happened to be within halloing distance of Springfield, they looked forward to hearth and home on the weekend.

There was one exception.

Riding the circuit in old Illinois,
One of the barristers, one of the boys,
Saturday, Sunday, the lawyers head home—
Saturday, Sunday, Lincoln's alone.

Home to their families, Davis and Swett,
Carrying stories and laundry, and yet
Wondering why their man can't come along—
Saturday, Sunday, something is wrong.

The work of the week in the courthouse is done,
The big house is waiting, mother and sons,
But Lincoln won't darken that door on this day—
Saturday, Sunday, Abe stays away.

The clown and the counterfeit stories are gone,
Only the shade of a stranger lives on,
We shrink from the sadness, we guess at his pain,
Saturday, Sunday, alone in the rain.

THE SHRINE OF DICKEYVILLE:
ELEGY WRITTEN IN A COUNTRY CHURCHYARD

On Mississippi's ridge I looked upon
A grotto wall dazzling in the sun
I could not take it in, could not go on
Until I knew by whose hands it was done.

. . . The priest had been a soldier, thus he knew
Not every country boy comes home from war,
And from that fact the bold idea grew:
A shrine to them and what they had died for.

(Jenamen and Loeffelholtz and Remenapp
Would not return to farm, or wife, or son—
Three boys who put their parish on the map—
Left lying in a trench in the Argonne.)

Untrained in Art or Sculpture he would start
A monument extravagant in grace,
The triumph of the longing of a heart
Which found its treasure in the commonplace.

With sand and cement and lime and broken glass
He stumbled on his way to the sublime,
Not knowing that his handiwork would last,
Or that he would be called before his time.

The lowly and the precious worked their weal:
Onyx, crystal, amethyst, and coal;
The fragile coral took on strength of steel—
The sum of parts would never match the whole.

Here is no fence, no keeper of the gate
To keep the passing sinner from the shrine;
Come joy or woe, come early or come late,
Through all Wisconsin's seasons it will shine.

continued on next page

Some kneel at Knock, and Lourdes they still surmount
To bathe, to chant, to seek some holy cure—
No miracles in Dickeyville they count,
And yet the pilgrims there are just as sure

The kindled colors of each rock and gem,
Quarried from all corners of the land,
Reflect the glory of God's diadem
As fashioned by a pastor's patient hand.

AFTERWORD: WINDOW DRESSING

In my poetry courses in college I was sold a bill of goods on what was then called "the New Criticism." The new critics maintained that a poem could and should be experienced in and of itself. The usual historical-biographical baggage dragged into the consideration of poetry was deemed at best a distraction, at worst a detriment to true appreciation and understanding. A poem must stand or fall or move or fly on its own merits. It is capable of taking on a life of its own beyond the earthly circumstances or even the artistic intentions of its creator.

The fact that I still subscribe to this extremist, existential theory makes it necessary to explain why I elected to include *my own notes* to introduce individual poems in this book. These notes are intended neither to explain difficult passages (I hope there are none) nor to narrow possible interpretations of the texts. They are, in most cases, merely my attempts to describe why and how a particular poem takes on life and shape.

By way of further explanation all I can say is that as a youth I took great pleasure from reading the little anecdotes Dorothy and William Wordsworth provided (many decades after the fact) for readers of his "Lyrical Ballads", and in my twenties I was grateful for the illuminating and contained commentary provided for each of Housman's lyrics in Dr. Joseph Mersand's Avon Library edition of *A Shropshire Lad*. In neither case did I feel the "background material" in any way cheated me out of any pure or personal reading of the poem at hand. I hope the same can be said by readers of my own casual commentary.

A good poem needs no introduction, and the childlike images of Wordsworth hardly call for serious parsing. Yet what a treat to be privy to Dorothy Wordsworth's inside story of a poem like "The Solitary Reaper":

continued on next page

It was harvest time, and the fields were quietly—might
I be allowed to say pensively?—enlivened by small compa-
nies of reapers. It is not uncommon in the more lonely parts
of the Highlands to see a single person so employed. The
following poem was suggested…by a beautiful sentence in
Thomas Wilkinson's *Tour in Scotland.*

And what budding—or aging—poet could not be interested in
Mersand's long list of notebook adjectives Housman *rejected*—
sunny, pleasant, checkered, patterned, painted—before settling on
the immortal "coloured counties" in "Bredon Hill"?

Although the epithet describes another place in another time, it
cannot help but remind those of us on the ridges and in the valleys
of western Wisconsin of our own favored place in the universe. If we
never see Ludlow or Alfoxden, it is no less lamentable that Housman
never looked down on Leland, or that Wordsworth never hiked the
Old Ironton Road.